MILLER'S

Advertising
Tins

A Collector's Guide

Robert Opie

MILLER'S ADVERTISING TINS: A COLLECTOR'S GUIDE
by Robert Opie

First published in Great Britain in 1999 by Miller's, a division of
Mitchell Beazley, imprints of Octopus Publishing Group Ltd.,
Michelin House, 81 Fulham Road, London SW3 6RB

Miller's is a registered trademark of Octopus Publishing Group Ltd.

Executive Editor **Alison Starling**
Executive Art Editor **Vivienne Brar**
Senior Editor **Anthea Snow**
Editorial Assistant **Stephen Guise**
Designers **Louise Griffiths & Adrian Morris**
Indexer **Sue Farr**
Production **Rachel Staveley**

Jacket photography **Steven Tanner**

The publishers will be grateful for any information that will assist them in
keeping future editions up to date. Although all reasonable care has been
taken in the preparation of this book, neither the publishers nor the compilers
can accept any liability for any consequence arising from the use thereof,
or the information contained therein.

ISBN 1 84000 067 8

A CIP catalogue record for this book is available from the British Library

Set in Bembo, Frutiger and Shannon
Colour reproduction by Vimnice Printing Press Co. Ltd., Hong Kong
Produced by Toppan Printing Co., (HK) Ltd.
Printed and bound in China

contents

Introduction

Tins are great survivors, kept as containers, as mementos of holidays or royal events, or simply because the finely crafted tin is a beautiful object in its own right. As with many collectable objects, once you start

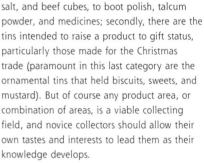

looking for advertising tins they seem to be everywhere – part of the fun of collecting them. Not only were they produced in such large quantities that numerous examples still exist today, but they were also used for such diverse products, and by so many companies, that there is a seemingly inexhaustible list of tins to find, and a collection can be formed relatively cheaply.

If condition is not an important consideration, then more unusual tins can also be acquired at reasonable prices. For instance, it is quite possible to find a tin with a lid that is in poor condition, in which case it will display well from the side and the damaged top will not be seen. Some tins, on the other hand, have the same image printed on both sides of the lid; with a little skill a worn lid can be reversed, and the look of the tin will be much improved (it will not, however, be authentic).

The great variety of tins often leads to the need to focus on a selected area (although it should be noted that this guide only considers those with images printed onto their surfaces, as opposed to those with paper labels affixed to them). Tins tend to fall into two broad categories. Firstly, there are those that were used for household products, ranging from coffee, gravy,

salt, and beef cubes, to boot polish, talcum powder, and medicines; secondly, there are the tins intended to raise a product to gift status, particularly those made for the Christmas trade (paramount in this last category are the ornamental tins that held biscuits, sweets, and mustard). But of course any product area, or combination of areas, is a viable collecting field, and novice collectors should allow their own tastes and interests to lead them as their knowledge develops.

As for the tins themselves, fortunately for today's collector, packaging tins tell us what they contained and who the manufacturer was. However, there are decorative tins that have no such information on them. Most of these would originally have had paper labels attached to the bases or inside the lids, but an intuitive guess is now required to identify the contents (in the case of large mustard tins, there is an inner lid that acts as a clue to the tin's original purpose).

The date of a tin can be even more difficult to decide. Apart from books – such as those of Michael Franklin on biscuit tins (see p.61 – **What to read**) – and manufacturers' own literature (which is often difficult to find), the tins themselves sometimes provide a number of clues that will help the collector to determine their approximate dates.

A coat of arms will indicate who was on the throne when a tin was produced, and you can borrow a book on heraldry from the library to clear up any confusion (the addition of "to the late", however, will only suggest a date after the monarch in question died). Design can also offer a clue to the date of a tin. Art Nouveau features, for example, can be found on tins dating from 1898 to 1910, when Arts and Crafts design took over; Art Deco-influenced design was current from 1925 until the end of the 1930s. During the 1940s war and austerity conditions left their mark – tins used inferior metals that now display thin wire-like marks of rust. Typical 1950s images feature the bright colours of the Festival of Britain era (1951) and the imagined attractions of the dawning space age.

Once a tin has been bought, identified, and dated, the question of maintaining it arises. A dirty tin will soon be restored to its former glory with a little cleaning, and each collector will have his or her own preferred method, generally using a metal polish or restorer. For collectors attempting to clean tins for the first time, it is worth experimenting with examples that are of no real value. And before restoring a valuable tin, it is important to test a small area that is less likely to be seen.

With experience it is possible to know which tins are likely to be cleaned easily – usually those with "depth" of printing. Early transfer-printed tins, and tins from the 1920s and 1930s with "thin" printing quality, need to be cleaned with great care and very little pressure. A light application of wax polish may help to bring out a tin's colours, but on no account use varnish, as this will reduce the value of a tin.

Most tins will suffer some superficial rusting on the inside, but as long as it does not appear active this need not be of great concern. Serious rust needs to be removed with wire wool, and this again should be approached with caution. The general rules for tins are the same as for most collectable items: keep away from direct sunlight, and do not display in humid rooms such as the kitchen or bathroom.

If you follow these few guidelines – whether you collect tins for their decorative appeal, or out of nostalgia for a time before supermarkets – the reward should be lasting pleasure, and, with luck, many an enjoyable discovery.

Prices and dimensions

Condition is a major factor when deciding the value of a tin. The price ranges given in this book are intended to reflect the value of a tin that is in "good" rather than "mint" condition. Prices for tins also vary according to geographical location and other market trends; as a result the price ranges given throughout this book should be seen as guides to value only.

Dimensions are given in both centimetres and inches. Tins are not shown to scale.

Early tins

The manufacture of tins as containers began in the early 19thC, when they held products such as varnish, biscuits, matches, and tooth powder. The problem of printing on tin meant that initially containers could only be embossed in order to promote their contents, or, as on one occasion, to celebrate the wedding of Queen Victoria and Prince Albert in 1840 (on the lid of a tin for metal paste). One obvious and simple alternative was to paste a printed paper label onto a tin. Occasionally, manufacturers would solder thin metal labels to their tins, as was the case with some Fortnum & Mason tea containers.

Huntley & Palmers biscuit tin, 1868, £90–110

▲ The Ben George tin
The tin above is remarkable for being one of the first to have been colour printed through the transfer printing process (see p.9), a technique patented by Benjamin George, whose tins were marked "Ben George, Patentee, London". This example was commissioned by Huntley & Palmers when the firm became supplier of biscuits to the Royal Household. The decoration was created by the eminent designer Owen Jones (1809–1874).

Bryant & May vesta tin and a coffee tin made under the "B&M pat" (Bryant & May patent), c.1880, £30–40 each

▼ Direct printing
A method of printing directly onto tin had been developed and was in use by the mid-1860s. The problem with the process was that it was limited for the most part to printing in one colour (usually black) onto a base colour (usually gold lacquer), although some intricate and attractive designs were produced despite the restrictions (a further colour could be added, but at the risk of its being out of register). Colourful paper labels were used, which added to the overall effect.

Storage tin, printed by J.H. Wilson, Leeds, c.1880, £30–35

▼ ► Transfer printing

By the end of the 1860s the transfer printing process had been developed, whereby a lithograph printed in reverse onto a thin paper sheet was transferred under pressure to the tin plate. French printers had achieved some success with the process, which was then improved in Britain and patented by a London printer, Benjamin George. Transfer-printed tins can be recognised because they tend to display a "crackling" effect like that seen on paintings (for another example of a transfer-printed tin see p.18 – Carr's "Jubilee", 1887, printed by Hudson

Scott). The tin below, which has an added colour paper label, was produced under the Bryant & May patent. The transfer printing method was followed by the development of offset lithography, which was patented in 1875. It was this process (and then chromolithography) that was to have the greatest impact on tin printing. Within 15 years almost all tins were printed using this method.

▼ Printing firms

The pre-eminent firm in the field of direct printing was the Tin Plate Decorating Company of Neath, South Wales, which made the example below. Tin box makers Huntley, Boorne & Stevens gained the offset lithography patent in 1878; with the biscuit company Huntley & Palmers as its main customer, the firm was able to establish itself as the leading tin printers. When Huntley, Boorne & Stevens' patent on the lithographic process lapsed in 1889, other leading printers took up the method, including Hudson Scott and Barringer, Wallis & Manners. (See p.61.)

James' French Blue tin, c.1880, **£30–40**

Walter Williams & Co. French Coffee tin, c.1885, **£30–40**

Food tins

With such a vast array of foodstuffs on the market, it is not surprising that every type of packaging has been employed to contain them. Paper packs and cardboard cartons have been predominantly used for products such as jelly crystals, semolina, cornflour, pudding mixes, and all manner of dried goods, including sugar and tea. Jars, pots, and bottles have been used to hold less solid products, such as jams, pickles, sauces, and pastes, while vegetables, fruit, soups, meats, and so on, have all been canned. Tins have been used for a wide range of goods, some with paper labels and some with directly printed surfaces.

Ling-Ford Baking Powder tin, c.1900, **£40–50**

◄ **Baking powder**
Baking powder, an essential ingredient of bread, pastry, scones, and cakes, was sold in packets for smaller quantities, while tins were used for larger amounts that had to be kept dry (although 4oz (113g) tins were not uncommon; Aero baking powder, for example, was sold in 4oz tins that had a picture of a biplane on the front). Joseph Lingford was established in 1861, making products such as liver salt and baking powder, with each pack displaying the company's trade mark: a girl carrying her shopping across a stream.

▼ **Custard powder**
The wife of Alfred Bird suffered with digestive problems and was allergic to eggs, so, having created a yeast substitute, he turned his attention to eggless custard powder. Perfected by the mid-1840s, Bird's custard powder was originally packed in card boxes, while card drums were first used c.1915 (although the first drum was of tin and had a patent measure – a depression for measuring the powder – in the lid). However, during the 1920s and 1930s most competitive brands were sold in tins; the illustration on the example seen here, which dates from c.1915, was modified over time.

Quorn custard powder tin, c.1915, **£35–45**

Wilton's Spices tin, c.1905,
£30–40

▲ Spices
Spices of every type were usually sold in small cartons or tins with paper labels – it was unusual for a company to go to the expense of a fully decorated tin. This large spice tin (19.5ins (50cm) in length), produced for Wilton of Doncaster (est.1853), was probably made as a gift item for the Christmas trade.

▼ Smith's Potato Crisps
Launched in 1920, Smith's Potato Crisps soon proved popular at parties and with picnickers. In 1922 the famous blue paper twist of salt was added to the 2d (1p) packet of crisps. Large square tins containing 18 packets of crisps were supplied to retailers, and by the 1930s smaller tins could be bought by their customers.

Force
Every so often, a food brand always packed in a paper carton turns up in a tin. Force toasted wheat flakes, for example, were first sold in Britain in 1902 and always came in packets, but nonetheless tins do exist – the question is "why?". Were they given out at exhibitions, or as promotional offers, being airtight tins in which the cereal could be kept (the latter was the case with Weetabix in the 1930s)? Some firms used tins instead of packets for export, as Rowntree's did with the Black Magic chocolate brand.

▼ Egifri
Most foods did not warrant the additional cost of a tin, but the manufacturer of Egifri must have felt that the product would benefit from a superior finish.

A substitute for egg and breadcrumbs, Egifri was claimed to be cheaper, more palatable, and easier to digest "by even the most delicate appetites".

Smith's Potato Crisps tin, c.1930s, £15–20

Egifri tin, c.1925, £15–20

Baby food

In response to the needs of Victorian mothers, an industry developed to cater for the demand for processed baby food. Mellin's Food, for example, was a substitute for mother's milk and was sold in jars, while Mellin's Food Biscuits came in tins; Allen & Hanbury used large green tins for its rusks. Virol had been packaged since 1899 in jars, but in the 1920s Virol & Milk was launched and sold instead in tins. Milk food was manufactured and supplied in tins by Glaxo and Cow & Gate.

Frame Food sample tin with advertisement lid, *c.*1910, **£20–30**

Cerebos Salt

An invention of the chemist George Weddell, Cerebos Salt first appeared in tins in 1894. The Victorian design was modified over time, becoming progressively blue. The famous "patent pourer" had been added by the 1920s, and a panel on the reverse of the tin showed the pourer in action. In the 1930s this panel was replaced by the company's trade mark: a boy chasing a chicken (this image came from Birdcatcher Salt, a firm that had been bought by Cerebos Limited in 1906).

Cerebos Salt tin, *c.*1900, **£15–20**

Bisto

Launched in 1910 by Cerebos Limited, Bisto competed with the products of many other gravy salt manufacturers, such as the Birmingham Food Supply Company (with Queen's Gravy Salt), Burdall, W.F. Hampshire (with Luxona), Symington, Pearce Duff, and Scott & Turner (with Tasto). In 1919 the artist Will Owen was employed to create the "Bisto kids", who in their first incarnation appeared on the side of the two largest tins along with the now familiar slogan "Ah! Bisto". (Smaller quantities of Bisto were sold in packets rather than tins.)

Bisto tin, 1930s, **£60–70**

▼ Edwards' Desiccated Soup

Edwards' Desiccated Soup, made by Frederick King & Co. of London & Belfast, was one of the most heavily advertised brands c.1900. The soup was sold in penny packets, in cylindrical and square tins with labels, and in square tins that were directly printed with the firm's red livery. S.H. Benson, one of the new professional advertising agents (previously, anyone with usable space to sell – news vendors, railway companies, and so on – could consider themselves agents), promoted the product with giant hoarding posters and shop displays, and sales were huge until ready-made canned soups gained the upper hand in the 1920s and 1930s.

▼ Oxo

Baron Justus von Liebig (1803–73) developed a concentrated form of meat extract in 1847, and in the 1860s a vast surplus of meat in South America allowed his research to be put to use, with Liebig's Extract arriving in Britain in 1865. Around 1900 the name was changed to Lemco and then quickly to Oxo. In 1910 Oxo in Cubes was launched – each cube coming wrapped in a tiny card box. Then in the late 1950s technology made possible a reversal of sorts, with each cube now being wrapped in metal foil so that a box could hold the cubes.

Meat cubes

The success of Oxo inspired many imitators, including Beefex, Erinox, Exox, Fam, Jardox, Ju-vis, Melbo, Oxeen, Silvox, Torox, Unitox, and Vigoral, along with Allies Brand beef tea cubes, Brooke Bond's beef cubes, Brand's savoury meat lozenges, and Valentine's Valtine meat globules. Oxo (previously called Liebig's Extract) also suffered from copycat branding (Liebig beef cubes and Baron Liebig's cubes both came in tins without any address). Soup was also produced in cube form, brands include Ivelcon, Buvo, Crosse & Blackwell, Gong, and Bifti (the last two being made by the company that produced Oxo); and there were Marmite cubes for "a delicious and nourishing food drink".

Edwards' Desiccated Soup tin, c.1920, **£10–15**

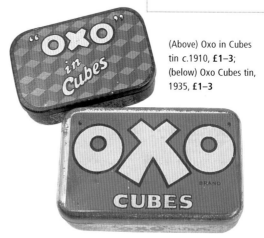

(Above) Oxo in Cubes tin c.1910, **£1–3**; (below) Oxo Cubes tin, 1935, **£1–3**

Mustard tins

The first mustard-producing company to flourish was Keen's, its factory having been set up in 1742 (and the association of Keen's with mustard was strong enough for the phrase "as keen as mustard" to establish itself). The story of Colman's Mustard began in 1814 when Jeremiah Colman (*d*.1851) moved his milling business to a flour and mustard mill near Norwich. Most mustard during the 19thC was distributed in oak casks which, from the 1850s, bore round labels for identification, and at this time there is also evidence of mustard being sold in tins with paper labels from 6lbs (2.7kg) down to ¼lb (113g). Colman's introduced its "penny" and "tuppenny" oval mustard tins in 1886.

Lion's Head Mustard tin, c.1885, **£25–35**

▶ Standard tins

Most mustard tins had paper labels that wrapped around the sides, and the colour, for obvious reasons, was predominantly a mustard yellow. Apart from Colman's and Keen's, a number of other firms supplied mustard, such as Champion's, Farrow's, Moss, Rimmington, and Sadler's. Occasionally, mustard firms would have the "label" printed directly onto the sides of the tin, as with this example from Barringer's, which has the Lion's Head trade mark. The gold medal awarded at the Adelaide Exhibition of 1881 can be seen on the side.

▼ Christmas tins

From the 1880s until the 1930s, decorative tins were produced by mustard firms for the Christmas trade, holding 4lbs, 5lbs, or 6lbs (1.8kg, 2.2kg, or 2.7kg) of mustard. Large households could easily accommodate such quantities of mustard in the days before refrigeration was common and the taste of meat often needed to be disguised. A wide range of subjects was found on the surfaces of the tins; this Keen's tin depicts "a national game" on its lid, and scenes from the British Empire – Australia, India, South Africa, and the West Indies – on the sides.

Keen's Mustard tin, c.1890, **£120–140**

Moss, Rimmington Mustard tin, c.1890, £110–130

◀ Prime ministers
This tin depicts the important politicians of Queen Victoria's reign. Gladstone, Chamberlain, and the Marquis of Salisbury (Robert Cecil) – all prime ministers – along with Sir George Balfour, are the key figures; on the corners were eight other men, including Randolph Churchill.

▼ Small decorative tins
Whereas Colman's and Keen's (later Keen Robinson, and then taken over by Colman's in 1903) produced large tins at Christmas, more modestly sized tins were sold by firms such as Champion's, Farrow's, and Moss, Rimmington (the latter also produced larger sizes). Farrow's in particular had some spectacular tins made for its mustard, such as the two seen here, which were aimed at children with scenes from *Who Killed Cock Robin?* and *This Little Piggy Went to Market*.

Farrow's Mustard tins, c.1895, £60–75 each

Subjects
The subjects on the sides of mustard tins tend to revolve around a number of themes: countries (England, Ireland, Scotland, or the British Empire – Canada, Hong Kong, Gibraltar, India); people (from royalty to Admiral Nelson); the natural world (such as the scenes painted by Sir Edwin Landseer, 1802–73); or children's themes (*Aesop's Fables* to *Little Red Riding Hood*). Later tins possessed less artistic merit and sometimes no pictorial element at all.

◀ Colman's
Christmas tins were produced for Colman's between 1880 and 1939; the Victorian tins were of the highest quality, but Christmas tins seem to have become less popular

Colman's Mustard tin, c.1895, £75–90

since Edwardian times, and the high point is arguably the 1898 Christmas tin featuring the Art Nouveau designs of the Czech Alphons Mucha (1860–1939). On many tins little prominence was given to the Colman's name, while others emphasised it to its best advantage, as does this example, which also bears the bull's head trademark (first used in 1855).

Biscuit tins

The ship's biscuit had become part of the staple diet on long sea voyages during the 18thC. Both Captain Cook and Admiral Nelson urged suppliers to create more nutritious biscuits, and also to find ways of keeping the biscuits dry and free from weevils. The answer was to pack the biscuits in wooden crates lined with tin. As the ship's biscuit became more palatable, so the taste for biscuits came ashore, and by the 1840s "fancy biscuits", as they were known, were making their way into polite society; by the middle of the century they were being exported to many parts of the world. It was during the 1870s that the decorative biscuit tin began to appear.

▼ Peek, Frean & Co.
The firm of Peek, Frean & Co. was formed in 1857 by James Peek, a retired tea merchant. Wanting to secure a future for his two sons, he persuaded George Frean to set up a factory in London making ship's biscuits. The Peek sons soon lost interest, but James persisted in the venture. He was joined in 1860 by John Carr (his elder brother – see right – ran the family biscuit company in Carlisle), and five years later he developed the Pearl biscuit, considered the forerunner of today's biscuit.

Peek, Frean biscuit tin, c.1877, **£50–65**

▼ Carr & Co.
In 1831 Jonathan Carr set up a small baker's shop in Carlisle. Within a year he had opened his own flour mill and bakery, which produced hand-made biscuits. In 1841 Carr was granted a Royal Warrant as biscuit-maker to Queen Victoria, and then in 1849 automation arrived – a printing press was adapted to take dough instead of paper, stamping out alphabet biscuits rather than words. The tin seen here depicts the royal residences of Windsor Castle, Balmoral, Osborne, and Holyrood.

Carr's "Jubilee" biscuit tin, 1887, **£90–110**

▼ Huntley & Palmers

The partnership of Thomas Huntley (d.1857) and George Palmer began in 1841, when they were confectioners and biscuit-makers of Reading. The King's Road factory was opened in 1846, and in 1851 the distinctive "garter and buckle" trade mark had been prepared in time for the Great Exhibition held at Hyde Park, London. Following the success of the first decorative biscuit tin – which celebrated Huntley & Palmer's royal patronage, granted in 1868 – special tins for the Christmas trade were produced each year.

Huntley & Palmers "Agriculture" biscuit tin, 1888, £90–100

Jacob's "Butterfly" biscuit tin, 1894, £130–160

▲ W.&R. Jacob & Co.

In Ireland during the 18thC, the Jacob family started to bake bread and ship's biscuits. In 1851 it decided to diversify into "fancy biscuits", and when the business grew it moved its premises to Dublin. In 1884 George Jacob visited America and saw the success of the cracker biscuit; Jacob's Cream Crackers were launched the following year.

Book tins

Among the most successful and popular tins were the book sets produced by Huntley & Palmers. The first set, "Library", came out in 1900 (*see* below) – eight "books" bound together by a simulated leather strap. Next year came "Literature", in 1903 "Waverley" (eight books by Sir Walter Scott), and in 1911 "Dickens". Further book-related tins were produced by Huntley & Palmers, including "Bookstand" in 1905, and a tin that made a life-like single red book in 1930.

▼ "Library"

One of the most popular decorative tins produced by Huntley & Palmers, "Library" was issued for the Christmas trade of 1900. The titles of the "books" include "Poetry", "Travels", "Science", and "Essays", while the volumes carrying the name of Huntley & Palmers on their spines are entitled "Cakes" and "Biscuits" (there is also a pun on the origins of the partnership in Reading). The tab with which the lid is raised has been designed to look like a bookmark.

Huntley & Palmers "Library" biscuit tin, 1900, £170–200

Huntley & Palmers "Lusitania" biscuit tin, 1908, **£230–260**

▲ **"Lusitania"**
Some tins were produced only for export, and this Huntley & Palmers tin depicting the Cunard liner *Lusitania*, which sailed into New York harbour on her maiden voyage in September 1907, is one example. During World War I the *Lusitania* became a target for German submarines and was sunk in 1915, with the loss of 1,400 men, women, and children.

▼ **"Victoria Cross"**
Apart from sentimental, artistic, and floral scenes, and images from around the world, decorative biscuit tins occasionally depicted specific events. This early tin from McVitie & Price, for example, portrayed military episodes where individuals had won the Victoria Cross for bravery. Tins by Huntley & Palmers have shown, among other things, the Oxford and Cambridge boat race, and Tower Bridge, following its opening by the Prince and Princess of Wales in 1894.

Macfarlane, Lang "Yule Log" biscuit tin, 1910, **£120–140**

▲ **Macfarlane, Lang & Co.**
It was in 1817 that James Lang opened a small bakehouse with a shop in Glasgow. John Macfarlane took over the bakery on his uncle's death in 1841 and greatly improved the bread business. In 1886 the firm moved into biscuit manufacture, and in 1887 it produced its first decorative tin, which celebrated Queen Victoria's 1887 Jubilee (see p.44). However, it was about six years before the company began making tins for the Christmas market.

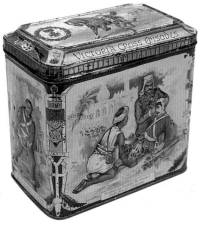

McVitie & Price "Victoria Cross" biscuit tin, 1893, **£130–150**

Huntley & Palmers "Egyptian Vase" biscuit, tin 1924, £70–90

▲ "Egyptian Vase"

Although for many years some designs had been influenced by the art and artifacts of the ancient Egyptians, when, in November 1922, two British archeologists uncovered the tomb of Tutankhamun in the Valley of the Kings, the treasures inside provoked great interest in Egyptian art. Huntley & Palmers designed a biscuit tin in the shape of a vase embossed with details of the pharaoh languishing in his palace.

▼ Shaped tins and toy tins

Throughout the 1880s and 1890s biscuit tins were being made into increasingly exotic shapes, becoming something of an art form in their own right. By the late 1890s a new trend had emerged for fashioning biscuit tins in the shape of everyday objects, such as baskets, pillar boxes, and luggage. By the 1920s an increasing number of tins that children could use as toys once the biscuits had been eaten was being made, including tins in the shape of a castle, a humming top, and a windmill.

Wheeled tins

Some toy biscuit tins have taken the form of vehicles with wheels. The earliest of these wheeled tins is probably the example produced for Macfarlane, Lang (it was known simply as "Motor Car") by Hudson Scott in 1903, which was then followed by "Fire Engine", also by Hudson Scott, in 1904. There were many other variations on the wheeled tin, including buses, coaches, trains, and delivery lorries. Toffee manufacturers also produced wheeled tins, although to a somewhat lesser extent.

Crawford's "Biscuit Bus" tin, c.1925, £2,000–2,225

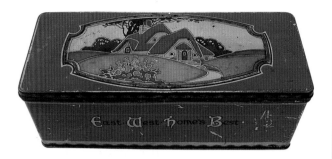

CWS biscuit tin, *c.*1930, £10–15

▲ Cooperative Wholesale Society

As biscuits grew in popularity, their production was soon to become an important part of the Cooperative Wholesale Society's (CWS) business in the 1880s. For its early decorative tins the CWS used the transfer printing technique, changing entirely to offset lithography by 1900. Novelty tins include those made in the shape of luggage trunks, pillar boxes, and telephone kiosks.

▼ McVitie & Price

A former Cadbury's salesman, Charles Price joined Robert McVitie in 1888, and a partnership was formed the following year. McVitie's had been bakers in Edinburgh from the 1850s, concentrating on biscuits since the 1880s (although oatcakes were a particular speciality). Having produced decorative tins since *c.*1891, McVitie & Price issued two "Kiddies" tins at the end of the 1930s, using images that were taken from two well-known books: *Sing a Song of Sixpence* (1880; illustrated by Randolph Caldicott) and *Tales of Peter Rabbit* (1901; written and illustrated by Beatrix Potter).

McVitie & Price "Kiddies" biscuit tin, 1939, **£40–50**

▼ Globes

Tins with maps of the world on them were produced in miniature by Rowntree's, on a larger scale by Victory-V, and as a novelty by Lyons' Tea. Two globes were issued by biscuit manufacturers: the first by Huntley & Palmers in 1906, and the second by Crawford's in 1938 (when the Munich crisis had created interest in world events and, as a result, the tins sold out immediately). The Crawford's tin – which was produced by the toy makers Chad Valley – was also sold as a toy without biscuits, and thus without Crawford's name.

Crawford's "Globe" biscuit tin, 1938, **£30–40**

▼ Cocktail time

During the 1920s and 1930s there was a great vogue for cocktails, which in turn led to a demand for snacks to go with them. In response, many manufacturers created cocktail assortments along the lines of Carr's Cocktail Canapés and Peek, Frean's Ritz Appetisers, Cheeselets, and, in 1932, the still familiar Twiglets.

Huntley & Palmers Cocktail Biscuits tin, c.1935, £34–45

Other biscuit companies

With the rise in the popularity of biscuits, it was not surprising that many bakeries added them to their ranges of bread and cakes. Some of the more enterprising firms also had decorative tins for their biscuits. Of particular note are "Greenhouse" (c.1905) by the Far Famed Cake Co., "Log Cabin" (c.1911) by Henderson's, "Concertina" (1902), which actually played, from Gray, Dunn & Co., and "Cheese Sandwich Inn" (c.1934) in the shape of a public house from Meredith & Drew.

▼ Miniature tins

While many decorative tins were replicas of everyday objects, the standard daily packaging for biscuits was also reproduced in the form of miniature tins, much to the delight of children who used them to play "shop", or in the dolls' house. While many manufacturers made miniatures, it was Huntley & Palmers who excelled at these tins filled with tiny biscuits.

Huntley & Palmers miniature biscuit tins, 1920s–1930s, £30–45 each

Confectionery tins

Until chocolate was taken up as a confection in the 19thC – and particularly before the advent of milk chocolate *c*.1900 – sweets were mostly based on sugar. But throughout the 20thC, chocolate creations have gradually eaten into the market for boiled sweets, toffee, butterscotch, and liquorice. Most of these confections were sold loose from jars or wooden boxes, being weighed out for each customer's requirements, but some manufacturers provided tins, and this enhanced the products' status as gifts.

Callard & Bowser Butterscotch tin, c.1896, £75–85

▲ Callard & Bowser
Started in London in 1837 by Daniel Callard and his brother-in-law J. Bowser, the reputation of this confectionery and bakery business was based on the quality of its butterscotch and nougat. From the 1890s it issued a number of flat tins of butterscotch, known as "children's boxes", illustrated with ducks, rabbits, kittens, and other animals. Further tins depicted the investiture of the Prince of Wales in 1911, and the leaders of World War I.

▼ Mints
A number of sweets were called "mints", or, in one case, "Mintoes", the latter made by Nuttalls of Doncaster from 1909. Fox's Glacier Mints were introduced in 1919, although the firm had been making mints in Leicester for many years prior to this. Sold from large jars or retailed in smaller jars and tins, Glacier Mints had established itself nationally as a brand by the end of the 1920s – promoted by vigorous advertising and a polar bear.

United Confectionery's "Marchatese" Mints tin, c.1915, £15–20

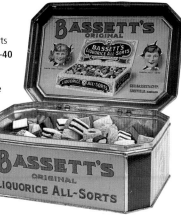

Bassett's Liquorice All-Sorts display tins, c.1925, £30–40

▶ Bassett's Liquorice All-Sorts

George Bassett founded his firm c.1842, describing himself as a "wholesale confectioner, lozenge maker and British wine trader". As with some other seemingly inspired ideas, the creation of Liquorice All-Sorts was an accident. The story has it that one of Bassett's sales team was in a meeting with a potential buyer when the tray of neatly arranged samples was inadvertently knocked to the floor. On seeing such an attractive mixture of liquorice and cream-paste sweets, the buyer immediately ordered some, and Liquorice All-Sorts have sold ever since.

▼ Pascall's Cuties

James Pascall had been an agent for Cadbury's before he set up his confectionery business with his brother Alfred in 1866. Early sweets included herbal cough drops, candy, and French rock, the range later being extended to barley sugar, sugar sticks, and almond rock. Pascall's was best known for its boiled sweets like fruit bonbons and its Weekly Assortment that included butter almonds, walnuts, and brazils, and fruit-centred varieties.

FACT FILE

Box versus tin

The concept of a gift box for chocolates had begun in the 1860s, when such delicacies were luxuries. In 1868 Fry's and Cadbury's offered decorative printed chocolate boxes for the Christmas market and then for the Easter trade. To compete toffee and boiled sweet manufacturers had to provide decorative tins – and they did exactly that. A tin of Tucker's Butterscotch from Totnes, for example, with a view of Torquay on the lid, could be bought as a seaside souvenir.

Maynards Fruit Bonbons tin, c.1930, £15–20

Pascall's Cuties tin c.1925, £30–40

▲ Fruit bonbons

All boiled-sweet manufacturers had their fruit bonbon confections. Mounds of ripe fruit were a popular design feature that gave immediate association with the many fruity flavours. Tins were used to up-grade the product to gift status, alongside toffee tins and chocolate boxes.

Mackintosh's "Nurseryland" Toffee
de Luxe tin, c.1930, £45–55

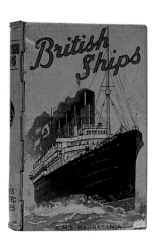

Walters'
"Palm" Riverside
Assortment tin,
c.1925, £50–60

Lyons' "Mauretania" tin,
c.1929, £80–100

▲ Mackintosh's

John Mackintosh
founded his business in
1890, at the age of
22. Just married, he
opened a small pastry
shop in Halifax that
also sold high-quality
confectionery. Soon he was
selling a new blend of toffee
under the title Mackintosh's
Celebrated Toffee, which in
1895 won a medal for its
excellence at the Industrial
Exhibition held in Leeds;
Toffee de Luxe, seen here,
was introduced in 1917.
A great variety of tins was
made for this brand, for
which the illustrator Mabel
Lucie Attwell (1879–1964)
created "Toffee Town".
Carnival Assortment arrived
in 1925, but was replaced by
Quality Street in 1936.

▲ Walters

Established in 1887, at Swan
Works, Poplar, London, the
company of N.B. Walters was
awarded a diploma of honour
at Olympia in 1913 for its
delightful creamy toffee.
Walters conceived the recipe
for Palm toffee, seen here,
in 1922. A range of toffees
followed, such as creamy,
fruit, walnut, brazil, almond,
banana split, and Tocolate,
and assortments such as
Fireside and Riverside.

▲ Lyons'

Around 1929 Lyons'
produced two series
of book-shaped tins
to hold assorted toffees.
One series of six had fairy
tales illustrated on the front
of each tin, while the other
showed British travel
achievements, which included
the railway engine *Royal Scot*,
the warship *HMS Rodney*, the
racing car *Bluebird*, the airship
R101, the seaplane *Supermarine
Rolls-Royce S.6.*, and the Cunard
liner *RMS Mauretania* (built in
1907, she had held the Blue
Riband for crossing the Atlantic
for over 21 years by the time
the tin was launched in 1929).

▼ Sharp's Toffee

Edward Sharp ran a grocery business during the 1870s and 1880s, and also made confectionery for the local area. In 1889 the first professional sugar boilers were installed. Kreemy Toffee was introduced in 1911, and the following year Super-Kreem Toffee. Around 1915 the macaw trademark was used, along with the slogan "Sharp's Toffee speaks for itself", and by 1920 the character of Sir Kreemy Knut was helping to increase sales, making Sharp's the largest toffee manufacturer in the world.

◀ Toffee firms

Apart from the toffee firms of Sharp's, Mackintosh's, Walters' and Lyons', there were many other well-known names, such as George Horner with his Dainty Dinah brand (and an endless stream of gift tins); Harry Vincent's Harvino Toffee, which was renamed Blue Bird around the time that the new factory was built in Hunnington in 1927; Farrah's Harrogate Toffee, founded in 1840; Parkinson's of Doncaster; Thorne's; Parker's; Lovell's, with Toffee Rex; Radiance; Edmondson's; Waller & Hartley, and Turnwright's. There were even Oxo Toffees, Bovril Caramels, Vitamalt Toffee from Boots, and Horlick's Malted Milk Toffee.

Novelty tins

Hundreds of confectionery tins have been made into novelty gifts. A particular favourite with toffee firms was the seaside bucket, which was issued in at least five sizes, ranging from 3½in (9cm) tall to 8½in (21.5cm) tall. Mackintosh's produced a set of domino tins and also a series of map tins, each having a map of a different part of Britain embossed on the lid. Around 1923 Sharp's Toffee created three "Kreemy Kottages" – the smallest is just 2in (5.5cm) across, while the largest measures 10in (25.5cm) across.

Sharp's Super-Kreem Toffee tin, 1930s, **£25–35**

Caley's Jazz-Time Toffees tin, c.1925, **£35–45**

Tea tins

The drinking of tea from China became popular during the 18thC, and by 1840 tea was coming in commercial quantities from India, followed by imports from Ceylon in 1880. Tea was seen as a luxury and was heavily taxed, although the tax was gradually reduced. When Gladstone introduced a significant reduction in the 1860s, the drinking of tea became steadily more popular; it was at this time that many tea companies, such as Tetley, Ridgway, and Horniman, were formed. The Cooperative Wholesale Society was formed in 1863, and tea became a leading part of its business. In 1869 Arthur Brooke opened his shop in Manchester, and Brooke Bond & Co. was formed three years later.

▼ Mazawattee

The trademark name of "Mazawattee" was registered in 1887. The name had been devised from the Hindu word "Mazathe", which means "luscious", and the Singhalese word "Wattee", meaning "garden". The name caught the public's attention, as did the brand's sentimental image. Used around the same time, this picture of a grandmother alongside her bespectacled granddaughter also found itself incorporated into the brand's advertising campaigns.

Mazawattee
Tea tin,
c.1910,
£23–35

▶ Gift Tins

Tea was sold in packets that were made up by the grocer, or, increasingly in late Victorian times, by the manufacturer. But some companies found that there was a strong demand for gift tins containing tea. Foremost among these was Mazawattee, which between the 1890s and 1930s produced a number of decorative tins; the subjects ranged from Queen Victoria's Jubilee in 1897, Edward VII's Coronation in 1902, and that of George V in 1911, to the stories of Dick Whittington and Lewis Carroll's *Through the Looking Glass*. Mazawattee also issued tins for its cocoa and chocolate business.

Mazawattee
Tea "Alice" tin,
c.1910,
£90–120

Tabloid Tea tin, c.1910,
£20–25

▲ Tabloid Tea

During the 1890s Burroughs Wellcome, a pharmaceutical company, created a compressed tea tablet called Tabloid Tea, which was sold in tins that contained 100 or 200 tablets. An early form of instant tea, Tabloid Tea was marketed with the pitch "Wherever you go – a good cup of tea", and claimed to be of "exceptional quality" and free "from stalk and midrib".

▼ Ellis Davies

Among gift tins, none could be more prestigious than that for Ellis Davies's Tea. On the lid is the company's founder, at each end the trademark, on the front the magnificence of St George's Hall, Liverpool, and on the back the frontage of the company's salesroom at 44 Lord Street, Liverpool.

Ellis Davies' Tea tin, c.1895,
£60–70

Tea-caddies

Traditionally tea was sold loose by the grocer, being blended to the customer's requirements, weighed out, and wrapped. To keep the tea fresh, it was transferred to the household tea-caddy. Originally made from silver, ceramics, or wood, by the end of the 19thC most tea-caddies were made from tin, usually with an image on each panel – buildings, animals, or the hero of the day. Many tins sold by manufacturers, even for products such as toffee or biscuits, were designed to be re-used as tea-caddies.

▼ U.K. Tea

The company trade mark of three glamorous ladies – who represented England, Scotland, and Wales – was used on many of the advertisements for U.K. Tea. The other sides of this tin show the Houses of Parliament, Balmoral Castle, and Windsor Castle. The lid depicts the archetypal Chinaman who is seen pouring out a cup of tea.

U. K. Tea tin,
c.1910, **£80–100**

Tins for other beverages

Apart from tea with its medicinal qualities "recommended by doctors to those of delicate digestion and sensitive palate", other beverages such as cocoa were applauded by the temperance movement. Many of the great cocoa manufacturing firms were started by Quakers or Nonconformists, whose righteous upbringing made them good businessmen, preferring cocoa to alcohol. Joseph Fry (1728-87), John Cadbury (1801–89), and Henry Isaac Rowntree (*d.*1883) were all such men.

Cadbury's Cocoa Essence tin, *c.*1885, £80–100

▶ Cadbury's

The origins of many large manufacturing businesses go back to a single retail shop. Such was the case with John Cadbury, who set up in Birmingham in 1824. His shop sold tea, and coffee, and cocoa that was ground by hand in a pestle and mortar. In 1831 a small factory was rented to help production, and ten years later the firm was producing sixteen varieties of drinking chocolate. In 1866 Cadbury's became the first British company to sell a pure, concentrated cocoa.

▼ Lutona

Cocoa was at the height of its popularity in Britain between 1900 and 1940. The English and Scottish Cooperative Wholesale Society had opened a factory in Luton in 1902 to produce cocoa, calling one of the brands Luto (it had tins with paper labels). During World War I production at the Luton Works increased by 44 per cent, but it declined in 1918 owing to the rationing of sugar (cocoa without sugar was unbearable, while tea served without sugar was drinkable). Lutona cocoa was introduced during the 1920s and sold in tins with direct printing.

Lutona Cocoa tins, *c.*1930, £10–15 each

▼ Coffee tins

The social meeting-place of the late 17thC was the coffee house, but when this fashion went into decline during the 1730s few households had the facilities to grind and roast the coffee beans. It was only in the mid to late 19thC that coffee-drinking extended again to the middle classes. While tea and coffee shops did local business, it was tea and coffee merchants who extended the distribution of coffee nationwide; Liptons, for example, had a chain of 400 retail outlets.

Ridgway's Continental Coffee tin, c.1910, £15–20

"Oxade" lemonade tin, c.1930, £15–20

Lyons' Pure Ground Coffee tin, early 1920s, £10–15

▲ Lyons' Pure Ground Coffee

The embellishments of the original Lyons' Coffee tin were modified throughout the 1920s and 1930s, until a "modern" image was devised c.1938. In 1940 an emergency blend was introduced – "This blend has been altered since some of the special types of coffee normally used are no longer available." Despite the wartime shortages, coffee continued to be sold in tins.

FACT FILE

Lyons

In 1887 J. Lyons & Co. started as caterers to the Newcastle Exhibition, before opening a chain of teashops in London. The first of these, which was in Piccadilly, opened in 1894. (The teashop waitresses became known as "Nippies", owing to their agility around the tables.) The company started to pack tea in 1905, and during the 1920s coffee, ice cream, and cakes were all sold as packed items – these items all went on to be distributed nationally. Lyons' Pure Ground Coffee (see left) was launched in 1920.

▼ Soft drink tins

A refreshing drink could easily be made by mixing lemonade crystals with water, and there was a time when drinks such as Eiffel Tower Lemonade, seldom seen over the past 40 years, quenched the thirst of thousands of tennis players (50 million lemons were used yearly to ensure supplies were sufficient).

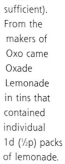

From the makers of Oxo came Oxade Lemonade in tins that contained individual 1d (½p) packs of lemonade.

Tins for household products

Tins have always been the most appropriate containers for household products such as liquid and solid polishes, and were often the only option for corrosive materials such as metal polish. In its time the tin has held a whole cupboardful of domestic cleaners: Bryterpol Car Polish ("for coach enamel, cellulose, fabric and woodwork"), Carr's Carpet Soap ("cleans and restores the original colours"), Duraglit Magic Wadding ("indispensable to the motorist"), and Hargreaves Linoleo ("also for cleaning golf clubs and gun stocks"). People were so familiar with metal-polish tins that there was some resistance to buying canned beer, which arrived in similar shaped tins in 1936.

▼ **Disinfectant powder**

During the 1870s and 1880s people were becoming increasingly aware of the dangers of bacteria, thanks to the work of people such as Joseph Lister. In 1877 John Jeyes, for instance, first sold a disinfectant fluid, and his Izal Fluid was launched in 1883; a disinfectant called Risco – "the most powerful germ destroyer known to modern science" – followed soon after. Made by H.N. Morris of Manchester, which changed its name to Dazzlo Ltd, Risco was also promoted as an insect destroyer.

Risco Disinfectant tin, c.1910, **£15–20**

▼ **Scouring powder**

Unlikely as it may seem, there were some scouring powders that came in tins rather than the cardboard canisters that have become the norm today. "Vim" was launched by Lever Brothers in 1904 and for several years the abrasive powder was sold in a tin. Shanks porcelain cleanser and the antiseptic cleanser Gospo, seen here with its trademark white cat drawn by the artist Louis Wain (1860–1930), also came in tins.

Gospo Cleanser tin, c.1920, **£25–30**

Salesmanship

How would you choose which polish to buy? Would it be one that sounded the most speedy, such as Quikko ("can be used to the last drop"), which had an aeroplane on the front, or the one with a promising brand name, such as Vericlean, Matchless, Glitterit, Eze or Shinio. But any car enthusiast would probably choose Venner & Prest's Headlight metal polish because a free polishing cloth was given with each tin – "see that you get it".

▼ Floor polish

Many had reason to be thankful for the increasingly effective waxes and polishes that came in flat tins with encouraging slogans. Lavendo, for example, "brings a delightful lavender fragrance to the home", and it was good to know that Mansion Polish was "excellent for the leather and coachwork of motors and perambulators". Just before World War I Johnson's Wax arrived in Britain from the USA; Samuel Johnson had devised the wax because, as a flooring contractor, he was continually being asked by his customers how best to care for wooden floors.

Johnson's Wax tin, c.1920, £10–15

Brasso tin, 1920s, £8–12, Bluebell Metal Polish tin, 1930s, £12–18

▲ Reckitts & Son

Reckitts & Son specialised in polish products, and acquired many smaller firms between 1903 and 1917. Bluebell came this way in 1908, as did Shinio the following year, ensuring that they no longer competed with Reckitts own liquid metal polish Brasso, which was launched in 1905.

▼ Boot polish

The Victorians mostly used liquid boot-blacking, which was messy, but the Edwardians had the benefit of solid boot polish in tins. Cherry Blossom arrived in 1903, when brands such as Nugget, Wrens, and Carr's Blackit were also becoming established; Kiwi arrived in Britain from Australia in 1912. However, none of these tins was easy to open until the "butterfly" opener or "winged" lever was introduced c.1930.

Frontier tin, c.1915, £20–25

Tins for toiletries

The images on the packaging of toiletries, cosmetics, and perfumes have always been destined to adorn bathrooms and boudoirs. Jewel-like tins add sparkle, as do decorative boxes of soaps and perfumes, and colourful labelling. In the 1920s, Pears launched its Golden Series toilet requisites, comprising gold tins of brilliantine, dental powder, face powder, cuticle cream, shaving sticks, and talcum powder. Not everyone could afford these products, and brands such as Robin Starch – which was promoted as an excellent nursery and dusting powder, and as a dry shampoo – were sold on the basis of versatility rather than sophistication.

Boots "White Heather" Talcum Powder tin, c.1915, £20–25

◄ Boots the Chemist

In 1877 Jesse Boot (1850–1931) took over his father's chemist shop in Nottingham, and a growing number of Boots outlets were soon selling goods at competitive prices, while "own label" brands were introduced early on. An extensive range of Boots tins can still be found – for brilliantine, throat pastilles, pine tablets, and iron pills, as well as talcum powders such as Devonshire Violets, Old Dutch, and Regal.

▼ Face powder

Although most face powders were sold in cardboard cartons, there have been exceptions to the rule, such as this tin, which was produced by Icilma. Other firms to use tins include Pears, with lids showing a lady in the act of applying her powder; Bell Sons & Co. of Liverpool, which produced Bienaimée Powder; and Breidenback's with Wild Apple Blossom Face Powder, which has a mirror inset into the lid.

Icilma Bouquet Face Powder tin, 1920s, £8–12

▼ Talcum powder tins

All of the toiletry companies, including Atkinson, Coty, Dubarry, Erasmic, Grossmith, L.T. Piver, Vinolia, Yardley, and 4711, produced talcum powder tins. The Potter Drug and Chemical Corporation of Boston, USA, extended its Cuticura skincare range of products to Europe in the early 1900s, and by the 1930s was well established in Britain. Cuticura Talcum Powder was illustrated on each side of the tin for adult and baby use, as was Cuticura Sun-Tan Talc.

Cuticura Talcum Powder tins, c.1930, **£10–15 each**

Nivea Baby Powder tins, 1950s, **£10–15** each

▲ Baby Powder tins

During the 1920s and 1930s, makers such as Cussons, Boots, and the United Drug Company (the producers of Tiny-Tot powder) sold baby powder in tins with illustrations of infants. However, it is Johnson's Baby Powder that has dominated this market since the 1930s.

Open and shut

For over a hundred years, those who have been involved in the technology of packaging have frequently pondered over the best method of opening and resealing a container. For talcum powder tins there was either a removable cap with the sprinkler holes underneath, or a twisting cap with holes that aligned with those underneath. Most talcum powder tins were oval shaped, but others were cylindrical, square, or triangular. Some could be even more unusual – a talcum powder tin by Dubarry had a square base that graduated to a round top.

▼ "Character" tins

Since the 1950s a number of talcum powder tins have been produced for children, depicting popular characters from film, television, or real life. These have included Andy Pandy, Captain Scarlet, Mickey Mouse and Friends, Scooby Doo, Sindy, and Tom and Jerry.

Margo of Mayfair "With The Beatles" Talcum Powder tin, c.1965, **£200–230**

Erasmic Shaving
Stick tin, 1920s,
£5–8; City Shaving
Stick tin, c.1920,
£12–18

Gibbs Brilliantine tin,
c.1920, £10–15

▲ Brilliantine tins

During the 19thC it
became popular for
ladies' and gentlemen's
hair to be rubbed with
Macassar oil – to the
extent that furniture
fabrics were required
to be protected with
"antimacassars".
By the 20thC the latest
unguent for the hair was
brilliantine, which, its makers
claimed, "stimulates growth,
renders the hair soft, silky,
and tractable". While liquid
brilliantine came in bottles,
solidified or crystallized
brilliantine came in tins.

▲ Shaving soap tins

The soap that we are familiar
with today was developed in
the 19thC, as was specialist
soap for shaving, which
started to become popular
during Edwardian times. By
the 1930s, although there
were many competitors, the
Erasmic shaving stick was
predominant. Sold in tubular
tins, Erasmic moved into card
tubes during World War I and
World War II because of tin
shortages. Bakelite was used
in the 1950s, and card boxes
from the 1960s.

Dr Scholl's Foot Powder tin,
1920s, £25–30

▲ Dr Scholl

By 1900 there were a number
of manufacturers producing
foot powders, some of which
were clearly aimed at soldiers:
Service, for example, with its
military slogan "Stand at ease!".
William Scholl (1882–1968)
had become aware of people's
foot troubles while working
at a Chicago shoe shop; he
founded his foot-care business
in 1904, and in 1910 opened
a factory in London.

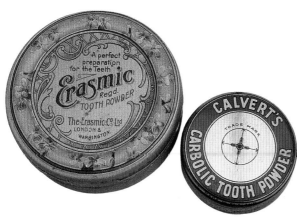

Erasmic Tooth Powder tin, c.1910,
£15–20; Calvert's Carbolic Tooth
Powder tin, c.1920, **£5–8**

▲ Tooth powder tins

By today's standards, few
people cleaned their teeth in
the mid-Victorian era, but
toothpaste gradually became
more widely available "for
cleansing, beautifying, and
preserving the teeth and
gums", as an early tin read.
Sold in white earthenware
pots, the tooth powder
needed to be mixed with
water to make a paste. By
the turn of the century, the
pots were being replaced by
tins. Ready-made paste in
collapsible tubes took over
the market in the 1930s.

▼ Smokers' tooth powder tins

Toothpaste manufacturers
understood that tobacco
smoking was not good for
teeth, and, as the popularity
of smoking increased, some
brands were aimed directly at
this market. Calvert's Tooth
Powder's sales pitch, for
example, used the following
line: "Smokers especially will
appreciate its tingling and
refreshing flavour."

Gibbs Dentifrice

From the 1920s to the
1950s the children's
favourite was Gibbs
Dentifrice, which sold in
a silvery aluminium tin.
It was promoted with
the line "defends your
ivory castles", and
children could scratch
their names on the back
of tins in the spaces
provided. In 1947 the
tins were coloured
green, red, and blue to
help children to identify
their own tins. The pink
cake of Dentifrice was
itself a feature: "The
little pink fairies bubble
up ready to clean and
polish the walls of your
ivory castles and frighten
Giant Decay away."

T.M. Smokers' Tooth Powder
tin, c.1920, **£15–20**

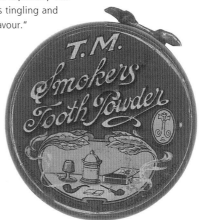

Tins for medicines

Every ailment needs its cure, and medicines have come in every type of container, from bottles and jars to paper cartons and pill boxes. But the tin has played its part in dispensing an extraordinary variety of pills, potions, and plasters, including Zam-Buk ("the great herbal balm"), Blood Salts ("composed of dandelion, horehound, and other blood-purifying tonic herbs"), Homocea ("instantly touches the spot"), ("stubborn chest troubles give way to") Roberts' Croupline Cough Lozenges, and Charleston Paste ("walking a pleasure, apply once daily, quite harmless").

Victory-V-Cough Chlorodyne Gums tin, c.1895, £30–35

▲ Victory-V

In Victorian times there was little comfort for travellers in cold weather. To the rescue came Victory-V gums and lozenges "for cold journeys", made by Fryer & Co. of Nelson, Lancashire. The firm also manufactured many other confections such as hospital lozenges and nutty caramels, and in 1865 was the originator of jelly babies. One of the first companies to use tins, it also filled novelty tins (which could be used when empty as toys) as an inducement for retailers.

▼ Allen & Hanbury

The firm of Allen & Hanbury dates back to 1715. It began as a manufacturing chemist, and its most famous product was Allenburys Pastilles (made of glycerine and blackcurrant). A great variety of pastilles was made, including Voice Jujubes – "a useful and agreeable stimulant before speaking or singing" – and throat pastilles, one variety of which contained menthol, cocaine, and red gum. Allen & Hanbury was also famous for its range of infant foods; its rusks, for example, were sold in large green tins.

Allenburys Glycerine & Black Currant Pastilles tin, c.1910, £3–5

▼ Health salt tins

The seeming cure-all potential of health salts, as invaluable aids to all forms of indigestion, "heaviness, headache, sickness, and giddiness", created a widespread demand. Many companies produced their own supplies, and some chemist shops had their own brands. By the 1920s there were perhaps more than a hundred different tins on the market, including Kkovah, Lingfords, Mineral Spring (which was "only equalled by the Natural Spa Waters"), and Ucal.

Scottish Cooperative Wholesale Society Health Salt tin, c.1920, **£15–20**

▼ Andrews Liver Salt

The partnership of Mr Scott and Mr Turner developed a health salt that "cleanses and imparts a vigour to the whole system and takes away that heavy and depressed feeling". From 1894 it was dispensed in penny packets, and in 1909 Scott & Turner registered the name Andrews Liver Salt and the design on the tin.

Andrews Liver Salt tin, c.1915, **£8–12**

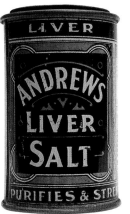

R. Parkinson & Sons

One of the world's largest medicinal manufacturers, Parkinson of Burnley, Lancashire was established in 1848. The company was renowned for its sugar-coated pills, which were dispensed in tins and boxes. During the 1880s and 1890s display tins were used by chemists to store Parkinson products, whether lung lozenges, head pills, or teething powders, and these tins served to promote the Parkinson company. Other products included everything from boot polish to baking powder and even honey.

▼ Elastoplast

During World War I the Hull-based firm of Smith & Nephew found that its products were in great demand. The company developed wound dressings in the late 1890s, when Horatio Nelson Smith took over his uncle's company. Elastoplast was launched in 1928 and sold in tins for the next 50 years. There have also been many other adhesive plasters sold in tins, such as Band-Aid (by Johnson & Johnson's), Dazlo, Golfix, and Mathaplast.

Elastoplast tin, 1930s, **£2–4**

Tobacco tins

During the 17thC the importing of tobacco from North America grew steadily, and by the 1880s there were 570 licensed tobacco manufacturers. At this time great advances were being made in the development of airtight tobacco tins. The most ingenious and successful tin was invented by G.H. Williams; it was cylindrical, and, when the lid was revolved, an inbuilt cutter pierced the inner foil. Such tins had paper labels; although some of the standard tobacco tins also had paper labels, most had the labelling printed directly onto the tin. With so many manufacturers producing their own ranges of tobaccos, it is not surprising that there were hundreds of different designs on the tins.

Hignett's Cavalier tin, c.1905, **£40–50**

▶ **Cavalier**
Tobacco companies vied with each other for custom, and sought to give their brands powerful images. The prestige of the firm could be measured by the number of medals awarded at the international exhibitions that were held regularly around the world. For example, the front and reverse of a medal were prominently displayed on Hignett's Cavalier Brand Bright Flake Honeydew, which won the only gold medal awarded at the International Health Exhibition of 1884 and the gold medal at the Liverpool Exhibition of 1886.

Hignett's Search Light tin, c.1900, **£50–80**; Capstan Navy Cut tin, c.1920, **£5–8**; Clarke's Thunder Clouds tin (with match striker base), c.1910, **£15–18**

▼ **Nautical themes**
With the tradition of sailors smoking tobacco (the term "navy cut" derives from sailors tightly coiling string around their duty-free allowance and then cutting off an amount when required), it was not surprising that many names and images drew on nautical themes – British Navy, Main Top, Royal Navy, and Sea Dog.

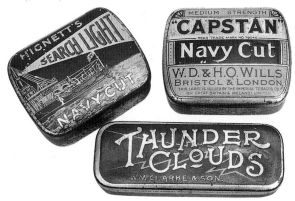

Wills' Main Line Flake tin,
c.1910, £200–250

▲ W.D. & H.O. Wills

With Bristol established as the main port for tobacco, it was not surprising that the city manufactured tobacco products. The origins of Wills can be traced back to 1786, although the name W.D. & H.O. Wills appeared for the first time in 1830. By 1847, when Wills produced Bishop Blaze and Best Bird's Eye tobacco, the era of branding had begun. These brands were followed by others, such as Black Jack and Old Friend, but tins of tobacco did not come into prominence until the 1880s. One example is the Main Line Flake tin (above); a later version has a red engine on the lid.

Player's Country Life
Smoker's Mixture tin,
c.1920, £100–120

▼ John Player

In 1877 John Player took over a Nottingham tobacco factory (and registered Nottingham Castle as his trademark). He had sold tobacco as a sideline for some 15 years previously. Country Life Smoker's Mixture, depicting scenes of fishing, cycling, hunting, and coaching on its tin, was launched c.1910 (the tin was also used to sell cigarettes). The "medium" variety, seen here, had blue borders, while the "mild" had red borders.

Gallaher's Honeydew tin, c.1905,
£25–30

▲ Gallaher's Honeydew

Tobacco tins occasionally depicted smokers relaxing in a social setting – Gallaher's Honeydew features a cosy gentlemen's club with its billiard room. This tin came in many sizes, ranging from 2½in (6cm) wide to 12½in (31cm) wide.

Cigarette tins

The introduction of the Bonsack cigarette-manufacturing machine in 1884 heralded a new era for cheap cigarettes such as Woodbine, launched in 1888. Before this time hand-made cigarettes accounted for a tiny proportion of the tobacco industry (and by the turn of the century, they still only made up 12 per cent of the market). Cigarette tins tended to be for 10 or 20 cigarettes laid flat, and therefore fitted conveniently into the pocket. Occasionally the tins were made more like cigarette cases, as were the tins for Lambert & Butler's Gold Leaf Honeydew, with 20 cigarettes. Tins were printed on both sides with the same design, and there were slightly curved tins to fit the hip pocket.

◀ **Promotional tins**
Cigarettes made an ideal gift, and manufacturers did, on occasion, have tins specially printed with company emblems. Since such a handsome gift would be kept, its promotional value proved to be worthwhile. Shipping companies, such as Hall Line – which stopped at such exotic places as Bombay, Karachi, and Marmagao – used this idea more than most. Few, if any, of these tins mentioned that they had once contained cigarettes – a tin for Seed's Hotels pictured its hotel at St. Annes-on-Sea and, inside the lid, two further hotels in Blackpool.

Muratti's After Lunch tins, c.1895, £45–55 (left); c.1925, £25–35 (right)

▲ **Muratti's After Lunch**
Collectors of cigarette tins have pondered for a number of years as to how many variations of Muratti's After Lunch tins exist. There are certainly eight major variants and further minor ones – it's all a question of "spot the difference": the wine bottle, the foliage, the plant pot, the fashion, and the moustache.

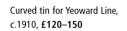

Curved tin for Yeoward Line, c.1910, £120–150

Neb-Ka tin, c.1905,
£35–45;
Miranda's Dream tin,
c.1925, **£55–65**

▲ Exotic blends

From Edwardian times there was a growing trend that favoured exotic blends of Turkish and Egyptian tobaccos. High society demanded something different from the daily cigarette smoked by the masses. Snake Charmer cigarettes from Salmon & Gluckstein (which owned 140 retail outlets in the London area by 1900) were made from Turkish leaf, and each cigarette was finished with a gold tip. By the 1920s, women were freer to take up smoking, and were targeted by brands such as Miranda's Dream.

Gaiety Girl tin,
c.1905, **£130–150**

▼ Girl power

The image of a good-looking female has always been certain to attract attention, and no doubt a number of Edwardian gentlemen found pleasure in having a likeness of a slightly risqué lady on a cigarette tin in their breastpocket. The firm of Cohen Weenen issued Gaiety Girl twice, with a different girl on each version. Stephen Mitchell's Woodland Belle was more demure in appearance, as was Taddy's Myrtle Grove beauty, who wore poppies in her bonnet.

John Player's trademark

FACT FILE

The famous sailor's head trademark used by John Player was bought in 1883 from the tobacco firm of W.J. Parkes of Chester, which used a sailor smoking a pipe to promote Jacks Glory. The lifebuoy frame was added in 1888. The two ships were added (but not always used) in 1891 when the design was registered. Variants were used until 1927, when the trademark was standardized.

Player's Navy Cut tin, c.1910–25,
£15–20

▲ Player's Navy Cut

Player's Navy Cut has been one of the most successful cigarette brands. Launched in 1900, the brand's packaging followed the graphic style of the "navy cut" tobaccos. The cigarettes came in a number of varieties, including Gold Leaf, Gold Tipped (which was "22 Ct Gold Guaranteed"), and Magnums.

Tins for every purpose

Tins were not only useful and often essential containers for perishable foods or corrosive liquids, but were also handy containers for all kinds of items. Sewing pins needed tins, as did typewriter ribbons, and, on occasion, other items of stationery such as paper clips and pen nibs. Tins that held more unusual items included one for a golf or slate sponge, one for Blakey's Family Boot Protectors, price 1s (5p) – "this box of protectors will save a sovereign" (a sovereign being a pound in "new" money) – and the one wishing its recipient "a happy Christmas and a glad New Year" from the Public Benefit Boot Company – but what would it have held?

His Master's Voice and Columbia needle tins, 1920s, **£5–8**; Aero-Needle tin, c.1910, **£35–45**

▲ Needle tins

As the popularity of the wind-up gramophone took off c.1900, so did the need for gramophone needles, which sold in small tins containing "approximately" 200 needles. The range and variety was immense. Many tins showed the horn-speaker gramophone on the lid, especially those for the famous His Master's Voice trademark with Nipper the dog, who first appeared on the tins c.1903.

▼ Tyre repair outfit tins

The development of the pneumatic tyre c.1888 created a demand for cycle-tyre repair outfits. With the craze for cycling well under way, the pneumatic tyre (which was the invention of an Irish vet, John Dunlop) was an instant success, since it did away with the uncomfortable solid tyres used at that time. The repair outfit contained glass paper, patch, glue, and ground chalk ("to prevent adhesion to outer cover"); these tins revelled in patriotic names such as John Bull and Britannia.

Express Repair Outfit tin, c.1910, **£10–15**

The Royal Scout's Delight tin,
c.1915, **£50–60**

Labelling

Tin containers have been used for every type of commodity – from the smallest of snuff tins to giant display tins, such as those used for Cadbury's Cocoa. For products as diverse as toffee, metal polish, salt, and talcum powder, "labels" were usually printed onto the tins' surface. With other tins it was more common to have a label stuck to the tin itself. Biscuit tins, for example, had colourful labels, although those produced for Christmas had direct printing.

▲ Writing set tins

The pride of every schoolchild was his or her writing set, containing an assortment of implements that couldn't be done without – pen, pencil, eraser, pencil sharpener, ruler, and perhaps also a pocket notebook and a painting set. Some tins were sold without contents (as some are today), while Callard & Bowser's toffee tins, having served their original purpose, could be used as pencil boxes.

▼ Motoring tins

The age of motoring took off after its embryonic days in the late 1890s, and since then a mass of paraphernalia has become available to every car owner (and tin collector). This includes not only car polishes, such as Reckitts Karpol, or car cleaners, such as Simoniz, but also petrol and oil. Foremost in this field was Shell, whose symbol has been in use since 1904.

Shell Motor Oil can, c.1930,
£40–45

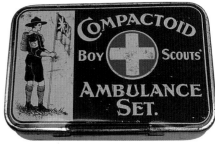

Compactoid
Boy Scouts'
Ambulance
Set tin, 1920,
£20–25

▲ First-aid kit tins

The handy first-aid kit was a must for every household, as well as every traveller, Girl Guide, or Boy Scout who needed to be prepared for emergencies. Boots Cash Chemists had its own Pocket Ambulance case with roller bandages, finger bandage, absorbent pad, lint, tape, silk ligature, sal volatile, tincture of eucalyptus, safety pins, camel-hair brush, and plaster.

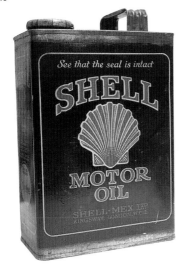

Souvenir tins

Many events, be they coronations or anniversaries, exhibitions or even wars, deserve to be commemorated – by mugs, plates, flags, and badges, souvenirs of all kinds, in fact, including commemorative tins. By the time of Queen Victoria's Jubilee in 1887, it was possible to produce finely printed and embossed tins, and since then many royal events have been celebrated in this way, including royal visits, marriages, and even the investiture of the future Edward VII as Prince of Wales in 1911. Many other occasions have been celebrated by images on tins, such as the voyages of great ocean liners – numerous tins, for example, depict Cunard's *Queen Mary* at the time of her maiden voyage in 1936.

Macfarlane, Lang biscuit tin, 1887, £150–180

▶ **Queen Victoria's Jubilee**
In 1887 Victoria had been queen for fifty years. Britain and the Empire celebrated her Golden Jubilee with many festivities. By this time the decorative tin was quite common, and biscuit manufacturers such as Carr's, Huntley & Palmers, and Macfarlane, Lang took advantage of this. Ten years later, for the Diamond Jubilee, the sweet manufacturers were also joining in the celebrations – a small round tin for Dunn's Chocolate Creams, and large tins for Callard & Bowser and for Parkinson's Butter Scotch.

▼ **Coronation tins**
Most of the tins celebrating the coronation of Edward VII and Queen Alexandra in 1902 were produced by the chocolate manufacturers Cadbury's, Fry's, and Rowntree's (Edward was taken ill with appendicitis, and the coronation was postponed from 26th June to 9th August 1902). Throughout the 20thC it has been biscuit and confectionery firms that have done most to commemorate royal events.

Rowntree's chocolate tin, 1902, £15–20

Hall's Duchess Assortment tin, 1923, £30–35

Fry's souvenir tin, 1907, £20–25

▲ **Royal events**

Following the success of the coronation tins issued in 1902, Fry's and Rowntree's in particular continued to produce commemorative tins for many other events attended by royalty, and often in what must have been fairly small production runs. Fry's, for example, produced tins to celebrate Edward and Alexandra's visit to Cardiff in 1907, and for the opening of the Royal Edward Dock in Bristol in 1908. Rowntree's even made tins to celebrate Empire Day, 1909, in Henley-on-Thames, and for a royal visit to the Borough of Accrington in 1913.

▲ **Royal weddings**

As early as 1889 there was a tin to celebrate a royal marriage: that of Princess Louise (eldest daughter of Edward and Alexandra) to the Duke of Fife. In 1893 tins celebrated the wedding of the Duke of York (the future George V) to Mary of Teck, and there were tins for the marriage of Princess Mary (George and Mary's daughter) to Viscount Lascelles in 1922, and for that of the Duke of York (the future George VI) to Elizabeth Bowes-Lyon in 1923.

FACT FILE

Royal events
Among those celebrated:
1887 – Queen Victoria's Golden Jubilee;
1897 – Queen Victoria's Diamond Jubilee;
1902 – Edward VII's Coronation;
1911 – George V's Coronation;
1935 – George V's Silver Jubilee;
1937 – Edward VIII's Coronation (which did not, in fact, take place);
1937 – George VI's Coronation;
1953 – Elizabeth II's Coronation;
1977 – Elizabeth II's Silver Jubilee;
1981 – Wedding of Prince Charles and Lady Diana Spencer.

▼ **Original contents**

It is not unusual to find commemorative tins with their original contents intact – be that coffee, tea, or chocolate. Souvenir tins were regarded as special and, accordingly, the contents might go unconsumed, while a gift from the monarch took on added significance (see p.48 – Queen Victoria's gift).

Cadbury's tin and chocolate bar, 1953, £5–8 (for the tin only; the bar has its own value)

▼ Seaside souvenirs

A visit to the seaside during the 1920s meant sand, sea, saucy postcards, and finding a souvenir – perhaps a piece of crested china or a tin of toffee, such as Palm Toffee, which bore the message "A present from Clacton". At the seaside town of Cleethorpes, Hancock's Palace of Pleasure provided all kinds of amusements, and illustrated tins of sweets to take home. Waller's toffee tins, on the other hand, featured a view of Blackpool's amusement park, and Hussick's Toffee decorated its tin lids with the famous poster in praise of a certain town's air: "Skegness is so bracing."

Thorne's Super Creme Toffee tin, 1926, £130–150

▲ Sporting souvenirs

When the Australian cricket team visited Britain in 1926, Thorne's produced a souvenir toffee tin showing the visiting team. It must have been popular, for this was the year that England won back the Ashes after 14 years, with a victory by 289 runs in the fifth test match at the Oval – an event worth remembering!

▼ Christmas souvenirs

Since most decorative biscuit tins were produced for the Christmas trade, it is rather surprising that not more of them incorporated seasonable themes – perhaps because the tin was to be kept and lived with as an all-the-year-round decorative item. Toffee manufacturers, on the other hand, were far less reluctant about putting Santa Claus onto tins, which then found their way into many a child's Christmas stocking.

Wintons X'mas Assortment tin, c.1930, £25–30

Hancock of Cleethorpes tin, c.1925, £25–30

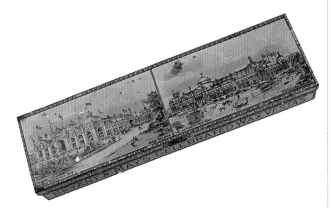

Bryant & May vesta tin, 1893,
£90–100

▲ Match tins

Since the beginning of the
19thC there had been tinder
boxes and, from the 1830s,
matchboxes made from tin.
Then, from 1878, Bryant &
May began to produce far
superior tins: for example,
the vesta tin for the Chicago
World's Fair in 1893, which
had two scenes on the lid
and two on the base. Having
perfected a new patent tin-
printing process, the firm
began to manufacture tins
for its own and other
companies' needs, and, as
a result, for almost every
commodity imaginable.

▼ Exhibition souvenirs

Exhibitions have, on various
occasions, been celebrated by
special tins, which were usually
issued by confectionery firms,
such as Stewart & Young of
Glasgow, makers of a souvenir
tin for the Scottish National
Exhibition held in Glasgow in
1911. The greatest number
of tins was created for the
British Empire Exhibition held
in London in 1924 and 1925
(the tin below is an example),
while only about three tins
were made for the Scottish
Empire Exhibition in 1938,
and not even that many for
the Festival of Britain in 1951.

British Empire Exhibition

The British Empire
Exhibition held at
Wembley, London,
covered a 225-acre site
and was opened by
George V in April 1924.
The various Dominions
from around the world
were represented in
permanent buildings.
Hundreds of different
souvenirs created to
commemorate the
occasion were available,
many of them tins.
Mackintosh's, Maison
Lyons, Riley's, Sharp's,
and Thorne's all had at
least one toffee tin for
their stands. Kenya
Coffee produced a
sample tin, Peerless
Erasmic a soap container,
and Rowntree's a
chocolate tin with a
picture of the Prince of
Wales on the lid.

Mackintosh's souvenir tin,
1924, £40–50

Queen Victoria's "South Africa" chocolate tin, 1900, **£25–35**

Hilton's Boots souvenir tin, c.1902, **£80–100**

▲ Boer War souvenir

The Boer War in South Africa came to an end in May 1902 after two years and seven months of fighting. During 1900 the sieges of Ladysmith and Mafeking created great consternation in Britain. The end of the war brought much relief and rejoicing, making heroes of the army leaders. A number of celebratory tins with pictures of the generals on the sides were produced by manufacturers at this time; this example features, among others, Lieutenant-General Robert Baden-Powell (the founder in 1907 of the Boy Scout Movement) and Lord Kitchener.

▲ Queen Victoria's gift

Queen Victoria made an unprecedented gesture when she asked for chocolate to be sent to her soldiers fighting in South Africa. Arriving in time for New Year 1900, the tins were designed by Barclay & Fry, with decorations added according to Her Majesty's special instructions. The order for 120,000 tins, each filled with a "½lb slab" (227g) of vanilla chocolate, was split between Cadbury's, Fry's, and Rowntree's. A present from the Queen was such an honour that many tins were carefully saved and still survive today, sometimes with the chocolate still in place.

▼ Princess Mary's gift

For Christmas 1914, during World War I, British soldiers fighting in France were sent brass tins containing cigarettes and tobacco, which were provided by Princess Mary's Christmas Fund. Also included in the tin was an envelope with a Christmas card that read "With best wishes for a happy Christmas and a victorious New Year from the Princess Mary and friends at home". Inside the cigarette pack was a photograph card of Princess Mary.

Princess Mary's cigarette and tobacco tin, 1914, **£20–25**

Rowntree's chocolate tin, 1914, £20–25 (without postcards)

▲ World War I souvenirs

Gifts in tins were sent to the troops during World War I, particularly in the first year when the full horror of war was not appreciated and there were not yet shortages of materials. Cadbury's sent chocolate in a tin that had George V on the lid and a card inside that read "With hearty Christmas greetings to the wounded soldiers and sailors, and with best wishes for their speedy recovery". Rowntree's produced a chocolate tin that had a sliding compartment underneath. The compartment contained six postcards with views of York or of the Rowntree factory.

▼ Home Front souvenirs

Many companies provided souvenirs of World War I, often with Earl Kitchener of Khartoum (Secretary of State for War) on the lid (he was drowned at sea in 1916 when his ship hit a mine). Confectionery firms led the way with commemorative tins such as Needler's Military Acid Drops and Barker & Dobson's Tipperary Toffee.

Callard & Bowser's Butter Scotch tin, c.1914, £20–30

Ridgways "Peace" tea canister, 1919, £20–25

Tin shortage

In wartime tin was, understandsably, in great demand, leaving little spare for tin boxes. During World War I, and again during World War II, cocoa tins were replaced by cardboard packs. In the 1940s, when shortages were particularly acute, even tin bottle caps were replaced by corks. While there were many victory mugs celebrating peace in 1918 and 1919, there were relatively few commemorative tins. Likewise, with victory in 1945, mugs were again made in number, but no tins were produced.

▼ "Peace"

During World War I, much emphasis was put on the comradeship between the Allies, and this was usually represented by the countries' flags or army uniforms. With the end of hostilities in 1918 and the signing of the peace treaties in 1919, a number of commemorative tins were produced. The "Peace" tea canister by Ridgways was one, and depicted the first attack by tanks, the surrender of the German fleet, and the politicians and generals of the time. On the lid were the flags of the Allies, with the symbol of peace in the middle.

Sample tins

An effective way of interesting would-be customers in a product is to allow them to try a sample. For generations this tried and tested method was used by the grocer, who would not only show customers the latest delicacy but also tempt them with a taste of the latest jam, perhaps, or a new flavour of cordial. As manufacturers began to pre-package their goods in individual units, prior to their delivery to the grocer, they also became increasingly aware of the advantages of distributing samples.

▼ Biscuit samples

As most biscuits were sold loose and weighed out for each customer's individual requirements, it was easy for the grocer to provide a biscuit sample. Nevertheless, it soon became equally important for biscuit manufacturers to impress upon the public the name of a particular brand. From Edwardian times a widespread system developed of sending samples through the post in tins. This practice was used by all the major biscuit companies (to a lesser extent by Huntley & Palmers). Sample tins may also have been given away by grocers.

▼ Tea samples

Most tea companies seem to have provided sample tins of their teas. Tins produced from the 1890s were the most colourful, while tins from 1905–20 tended to use embossed lettering out of a metallic printed surface. With the great Dr Samuel Johnson renowned as a "hardened and shameless tea-drinker", it is no surprise that Johnson Johnson & Co. used his likeness on its sample tea tins.

Macfarlane, Lang Rich Tea sample tin, c.1915, **£15–20**, McVitie & Price Digestive sample tin, c.1925, **£20–25**

Johnson Johnson & Co's Tea sample tin, c.1895, **£30–35**, Matheson McLaren & Co's Tea sample tin, c.1910, **£10–12**

Miniatures

There has always been a fascination with miniature versions of familiar objects. The art of producing miniatures was taken a step further when Rowntree's began to issue tiny objects formed out of tin and filled with cachons – everything from a coal scuttle and cricket bat to a penknife and a piano. Fry's and Clarnico did much the same thing, although neither firm used as many items.

Boots Regal Talcum Powder miniature tin, c.1920, £15–20

▼ Cocoa samples

As with tea, numerous sample tins were produced by cocoa firms, particularly Cadbury's, Fry's, and Rowntree's (they often decorated the lids of the tins with flags and coats of arms, such as that of the City of Liverpool for Rowntree's). Bournville Cocoa sample tins were also issued with some of the great ocean liners, such as the *Olympic*, on them. Other cocoa sample tins include Faulder's Cocoa, Ferru Cocoa, Thorne's Health Cocoa, and Dr Tibbles' Vi-Cocoa. Many of these tins could also be used as vesta boxes, since they had match strikers on the base.

Cadbury's Cocoa sample tin, c.1900, £25–30, Fry's Cocoa sample tin, c.1915, £20–25

▲ Miniature tins

Serving the same purpose as sample tins, but being small copies of full-size products, miniature tins were effective promotional gimmicks. A sample tin of Andrews Liver Salt, for example, had this inscription on its lid: "Here's health! With best wishes from the management", suggesting that these tins were to be used at the workplace. Huntley & Palmers also made miniature tins for many of their classic brands between 1900 and the 1950s, when they could be purchased for 1d or 2d (½p or 1p) each (see p.21 – Miniature tins).

▼ Miniature objects

Rowntree's produced more of these miniature tins in the shape of familiar objects than any other company – teddy bears, bananas, and Christmas puddings, to name but a few. Clarnico was more sporty, with tennis rackets and golf clubs, while for Fry's there were lanterns and cash boxes.

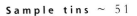

Rowntree's miniature cricket bat, c.1915, £60–70; Fry's miniature fob watch, c.1910, £100–130,

Gift tins

The free gift box was one of the great promotional ideas of the late-Victorian period. Purchasers of cocoa were invited to save up the coupons found in packs and, when they had the requisite number, send off for a free gift casket, which would arrive through the post, filled with chocolates. Cadbury's and Rowntree's were the two principal companies to offer gift tins, producing new examples each year. By the 1920s and 1930s the concept had been extended so that a whole range of useful gifts was available in exchange for cocoa coupons. By this time both the Cooperative Wholesale Society and Fry's were running similar schemes.

▼ Rowntree's gift tins

Among the first ranges of Rowntree's gift tins were those produced between c.1900 and 1908. The tins were flat, containing a single layer of chocolates, and there was a colourful image on the lid. In addition to the example seen below, the pictures were a girl with a St Bernard dog, a Regency lady and gentleman sitting on a couch, children at the seaside, an eagle, and a gentleman looking over to a lady on a bench.

Rowntree's "Shakespearean" gift casket, 1913, **£30–40**

Rowntree's gift tin c.1905, **£150–180**

▲ "Shakespearean"

By 1909 Rowntree's was producing gift boxes in a variety of shapes. In 1910 the "useful gift casket" had a handle, and in 1911 it celebrated the coronation of George V. In 1912 the tin had a detachable lid and base, in the panels of which were copies of pictures by famous artists that could be hung on the wall. In 1913 a "Shakespearean" gift casket was produced that contained a bookmark describing the scenes on each side, and that was "designed to represent antique carved ivory".

Cadbury's gift tin, c.1905,
£25–35

▲ Cadbury's gift tins

Cadbury's started its gift scheme in the early years of the century; the first series of tins featured scenes of the chocolate and cocoa works, "the factory in a garden" as Cadbury's described it, at Bournville, Birmingham. One gift-tin lid showed "a corner of the girls' recreation ground", and another "Bournville Lane"; both of them had pictures of the cricket ground and the men's gymnasium on the base of the tin.

▼ Imitation boxes

Many gift tins were made to look like wooden boxes. In 1914, for example, Cadbury's produced a Louis XV marquetry-style box, and in 1916 Bournville produced a "Cocoa Caddy" containing cocoa and a spoon that was a copy of an 18thC wooden example. The lid of the Rowntree's gift tin seen below is also a stand on which the base can sit.

Gift tins

Rowntree's gift tins were clearly popular: "Many thanks for the beautiful box of chocolates and pastilles which I received safely. They are simply delicious, also the box is so pretty that it will make a splendid ornament"; "We enjoyed the contents very much, and the box itself was quite a work of art"; "The boxes are more handsome than ever, and also more useful."

Cadbury's Quadriga gift tin, c.1913, £10–15

▲ Quadriga

It is ironic that just two years before the outbreak of World War I, the *Quadriga* sculpture by Captain Adrian Jones, which surmounts the Arch on Constitution Hill, London, was presented to the nation as a memorial to Edward VII. The *Quadriga* symbolized the idea of "The figure of Peace descending upon the Chariot of War", and the sculpture was embossed on the lid of this Cadbury's gift tin.

Rowntree's gift tin, c.1925,
£12–18

Speciality tins

The popularity of decorative tin boxes, the manufacture of which had developed into a specialized craft, led companies to use tin in all manner of ways in order to promote themselves. Advertisements were not only produced as posters, display cards, and leaflets, but also as magnificent tin signs. Many promotional items were also made from tin, such as money boxes, string-dispensing tins, and display tins. Further items made from tin included drinks trays, pin trays, and ashtrays. The durability of tin gave longevity to oddments such as Gossages' Dry Soap Sprinkler and Field's Ozokerit lighthouse night light holder.

Cadbury's souvenir tin, c.1935, £12–18

▲ Factory tins
The Victorians were proud of their "modern" factories, and incorporated them into many advertisements to show off the size of their premises. For many years, up until the 1970s, organized visits to factories were encouraged by manufacturers, and, at the end of each tour, it was customary to present the visitors with a sample of the factory's output. For confectionery companies this may have been a box of sweets, while Cadbury's and Fry's presented visitors to their factories with a special souvenir tin of chocolates.

▼ Vending machine tins
By the end of the Victorian era the vending machine had managed to establish itself as a convenient sales point, and it is not surprising that tin miniature vending machines were produced, particularly by chocolate manufacturers such as the Stollwerck brothers of Cologne, Germany. A number of different examples were also made for the British market – "for the obedient child" (as at least one read), who would get a miniature bar of chocolate in return for a halfpenny.

Stollwerck chocolate vending machine, c.1900, £150–180

▼ Savings bank tins

Much publicity was aimed at children during the rise of the branded product. Paper novelties, many of which were to end up in children's scrapbooks, were given out by grocers to their favoured customers. The savings bank tin was not only practical in teaching children the benefits of saving money, "a penny saved is a penny earned", it also served as a constant reminder of the product itself. Many of these "banks" came with their own keys.

CWS Cooperative Tea tin money box, c.1925, **£30–40**

▲ Money box tins

A number of money boxes were designed to resemble the product itself. For example, a can of salmon (with the label printed directly onto the side) could make a fun money box (although some of the designs made it quite difficult to extract money from the box).

Spillers Nephews biscuit tin savings bank, c.1910, **£100–120**

Pillar boxes

Many companies have produced pillar box money banks. Some of the first, c.1897, were for biscuit firms, such as the A.1. Biscuit Company and W. Dunmore & Son. Huntley & Palmers produced one in 1906, Macfarlane, Lang in 1910, and the CWS in 1913 and 1926. Huntley & Palmers made a "penny in the slot" biscuit-dispensing machine in 1923, and a standard pillar box ten years later. Rowntree's issued a "toffee" one in the mid-1920s, and Oxo produced one for George VI's coronation in 1937.

▼ Pillar box tins

The tradition of making Post Office pillar boxes into money boxes can be traced back to the 1890s, and every so often two companies would use the same tin but at different times and for different products. This street pillar box or "postal pillar", made by Barringer, Wallis & Manners, was first issued in 1913 and contained Cooperative Wholesale Society biscuits (the name was stamped on the base of the tin only). It was reissued about fifteen years later, but this time filled with toffees from R.S. McColl.

R.S. McColl toffee tin money box, c.1930, **£50–60**

▼ Tea-caddy tins

While popular from the earliest times of tin boxes, tea-caddies were rarely made as promotional items. Biscuit companies produced tins that were designed for use as tea-caddies, particularly during the 1920s and 1930s, but, as tradition dictated, without any self-promotion (see p.6 – Jacob's Floral Tea Caddy). In the mid 1920s Lyons' Tea issued four tea-caddies, each of which featured a different household item: a calendar, an egg-timer, a mirror, and (see below) a thermometer.

▼ String tins

In the days of customer service, many items were individually wrapped and the wrapping paper secured with a piece of string; for the convenience of the grocer, tins that held string were provided by many manufacturers. These tins were heavily weighted at the base and often had cutter devices at the top.

Dr. Tibbles' Vi-Cocoa string tin, c.1910, **£100–120**

▼ Promotional string tins

Promotional string tins had colourful advertisements for products blazoned around the sides. The products were mostly grocery-related items such as Brasso, Camp Coffee, Colman's Mustard, Health Cocoa, or Restu washing powder. Occasionally string tins were made for less-likely products, such as Stotherts medicine pills or bottled beer from Worthington's.

Lyons' tea-caddy tin, c.1925, **£25–35**

Peek Frean & Co's Pat-A-Cake Biscuits string tin, c.1925, **£70–85**

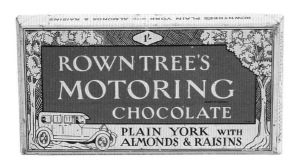

Rowntree's Motoring Chocolate tin with dummy bar, c.1925, £70–85

▲ Dummy tins

Until the 1970s, confectionery shops had wonderful window displays intended to tempt passers-by into making a purchase (sweet manufacturers often had whole departments given over to making dummy packs). To stop chocolate melting in the heat of summer, display chocolate bars often had blocks of wood inside the wrappers. Occasionally display chocolate bars were even made from tin.

▼ Tin advertisements

Unlike enamel signs or paper posters, tin signs could be embossed to good effect, and the colour printing produced a vibrant result. A number of speciality tin signs were also made, including finger-plates for shop doors that sometimes incorporated match strikers. Some companies also created quite elaborate displays to promote products, such as this for Fry's Chocolate Cream.

FACT FILE

Advertising with tin

Tin advertisements can create interesting and colourful displays when in combination with a collection of tins. In some instances these advertisements, or signs, will also add further background information about the product. Shop display cards sometimes have spaces for holding a tin or pack of tins. In such instances it is important to make sure that the date of a tin or a pack of tins corresponds (as closely as is reasonable) to the date of the display card.

Fry's Chocolate Creams tin display, c.1930, £110–140

Modern tins

Since the 1950s there have been many changes in the ways in which goods are packaged. The increased use of plastics and, to a lesser extent, aluminium foil has had a great impact on what the consumer sees on the shelves of a self-service supermarket. As a material, tin is relatively more expensive – talcum powder is now sold in plastic containers, and tins of sweets are less common. Nevertheless, or perhaps because of this, tins still retain their air of prestige.

▶ **Novelty tins**
During the 1980s and 1990s, a number of novelty tins were designed for certain brands of chocolate biscuits. Some of the tins also incorporate shaped plastic: Cadbury's "Spaceship" of 1983, which was filled with chocolate biscuit balls, and McVitie's Jaffa Cakes "Express" of 1985, which had plastic wheels. In 1983 a Cadbury's chocolate wafer biscuit tin was produced that took the form of a series of five books by Charles Dickens.

McVitie's Chocolate
Fingers tin, 1995, £2–4

▼ **Christmas biscuit tins**
The production of special tins for the Christmas trade came to an end with the outbreak of World War II. Although many biscuit tins have been made since the 1950s, their number and diversity have declined. In 1997, however, McVitie's produced a charming tin with an embossed lid on which a selection of its pre-war tins and promotional items was depicted (some names were altered by the parent company, United Biscuits, to read, for example, McVitie's rather than Crawfords).

McVitie's biscuit tin, 1997,
£1–2

Kiwi Shoe Shine Kit tin, 1996, £1

▲ Shoe-shine kits
Between 1905 and 1930 many shoe-polish companies produced shoe-cleaning sets in tins that would typically contain a shoe brush, a tin of polish, a cloth, and a buffer. Some tins were larger and could therefore include two brushes, and both black and brown polish. Cherry Blossom also added an tin advertising surface to its shoe brushes.

▼ Replica tins
Since the 1970s reproduction tins have been made that – particularly if they are little worn – often look very similar to the originals. In the early 1970s a replica was made of the Boer War tin with Union Jack background that looked exactly like the original, the diiference being that the modern tin was shiny. In the 1980s tins by Replican (which is marked on the back of the lid) included Cadbury's Cocoa, Colman's Mustard (see below), Oxo, and Typhoo.

Colman's Mustard tin, c.1890, £90–110 (left), Replican Colman's Mustard tin, c.1985, £3–4 (right)

FACT FILE

Storage tins
Some tins were designed so that when the product (Mazawattee Tea, for example, or sweets from Edmondson's) had been consumed, a set of kitchen canisters could be built up, the tins having "tea", "sugar", and so on printed on the reverse. During the 1950s paper stickers were provided.

Callard & Bowser storage tin, 1995, £3–6

▲ Storage tins
Empty tins have always been used as storage containers, one reason why so many of them survive today; many tins were designed to serve as practical containers once their contents had been consumed. In recent years, however, many have been sold purely as storage tins, without contents. The tin seen here features images from earlier Callard & Bowser tins (see p.22 Callard & Bowser).

Where to buy

Tins come in all shapes and sizes and are liable to be found almost anywhere. Most homes seem to harbour a few, even if they are in the garden shed full of nails. But for most collectors, it is the car boot sales, the collectors' fairs, and the antique markets that bring the most immediate results.

Many cities and towns have established areas where there is trade in antiques. In London, for example, the places to visit include Alfies Antiques Market (Church Street, London, W2), and the markets at Portobello Road (Notting Hill Gate, London, W11), and Camden Passage (Islington, London, N1).

Antiques fairs are held throughout the year and all over the country; they range in size from open air fairs, such as those held at Newark, Nottinghamshire and Ardingly, Sussex, to indoor fairs, such as those held at Donnington, East Midlands, and Alexandra Palace, London. Tins also find their way into a number of auctions.

What to read

Griffith, David: *Decorative Printed Tins* (Studio Vista, 1979)

Franklin, Michael: *British Biscuit Tins* (New Cavendish, 1979)

Franklin, Michael: *British Biscuit Tins* (V&A, 1984)

Hornsby, Peter: *Decorated Biscuit Tins* (Schiffer Publishing, 1984)

Opie, Robert: *Sweet Memories* (Pavilion, 1988; includes confectionery tins)

Opie, Robert: *Packaging Source Book* (Macdonald Orbis, 1989; includes tins)

Where to see

Few museums have displays given over to tins. The Victoria and Albert Museum in London, for example, holds Michael Franklin's collection of biscuit tins, but they are not on display.

Part of The Robert Opie Collection can be viewed at the Museum of Advertising and Packaging (The Albert Warehouse, Gloucester Docks, Gloucester). More of the collection will be displayed at The Museum of Memories (Wigan Pier, Wigan), which is due to open in April 1999. Reading Museum (Blagrave Street, Reading) houses a collection of Huntley & Palmers biscuit tins.

Tin makers & printers

The Tin Plate Decorating Company of Neath, South Wales, was established early in the 1860s (it had previously traded under the name of Sandford & Bird); the firm shared its premises with the tin plate manufacturers Leach, Flower & Company. Philip Flower and Wickham Flower had holdings in both companies and held patents (taken out in 1864 and 1869) for printing in a single colour directly onto tin. Not only was printing directly onto tin a problematic process, there were also complications to printing more than a single colour. Despite the fact that it had become the pre-eminent direct printer, it was not surprising that the Tin Plate Decorating Company turned also to transfer printing.

The principal exponent of transfer printing was one Benjamin George of Hatton Garden, London, who took out patents during the late 1860s (although it seems that transfer printing had been developed in France). The process entailed a lithographed colour image being printed in reverse onto a thin paper sheet that was then applied under pressure to the tin plate. Although transfer printing was in continual use until the end of the 19thC, its development eventually led to the next stage in the printing of tins: offset lithography (see p.9) – the standard 20thC method.

The first patent for offset lithography was awarded to the London printing firm of Barclay & Fry in 1875. Barclay and Fry lacked the finance to implement or develop the process, and the patent was bought by Bryant & May in 1877. Within two years the licence had been given to Huntley, Boorne and Stevens, with Bryant & May agreeing to finance new machinery.

In 1831 Joseph Huntley had set up as an ironmonger in Reading, in premises located opposite to a bakery owned by his brother, Thomas. During 1837 Joseph started to supply tins for Thomas's growing trade in biscuits. In 1841 George Palmer joined Thomas Huntley and Huntley & Palmers was formed; in 1864 Samuel Stevens and James Boorne joined James Huntley to form Huntley, Boorne & Stevens. The two companies merged in 1918.

Hudson Scott & Sons had been lithographic printers since 1799. In 1876 the firm began transfer printing on tin plate, supplying the local biscuit firm Carr's of Carlisle (see p.16 – Carr & Co.). When Barclay & Fry's patent for offset lithography lapsed in 1889, Hudson Scott, having already experimented with the process, was probably the first company to take advantage. When Queen Victoria sent 120,000 tins of chocolates to the soldiers in the Boer War (see p.48 – Queen Victoria's gift), it was Hudson Scott who supplied most of them.

In the 1840s Barringer had operated as a packer of various commodities, including mustard. By the 1860s, Barringer & Brown, as the company was now known, was selling mustard tins that were decorated with printed labels, or had been transfer printed by the Tin Plate Decorating Company.

Barringer & Brown became Barringer, Wallis. The firm was buoyed by the success of a new venture into tin making, which had been promoted by a partner in the firm, Charles Manners, and, in 1889, a separate company was formed: Barringer, Wallis & Manners. In the early 1890s lithographic tins were being produced at its Mansfield factory.

Index

Acknowledgments

Picture acknowledgments
All pictures copyright Robert Opie except:
Octopus Publishing Group Ltd./Steve Tanner **cover**, **2**.

Author's acknowledgments
With thanks to the following dealers for their help on pricing tins:
Steve Burton (various antiques fairs, including Newark, Notinghamshire)
John Emmett (Portobello Road, Notting Hill Gate, London, W11)
David Huxtable (Alfies Antiques Market, Church Street, London, W2)